NIb/06 RRE

NEW INSTANT for the CHURCH MAGAZINE

Illustrated by Arthur Baker, Darren,
Taffy Davies, Steve English
and Abigail Wakeling

Kevin Mayhew

Introduction

The demand for more 'instant art' continues to be so great that we are happy to present this collection of *New Instant Art for the Church Magazine.* Five different artists have produced a wide range of material covering a multitude of themes, and all with the needs of our regular users very much in mind. The 46 pages of high-quality photocopiable artwork and puzzles will be an asset to editors of a variety of church publications.

Readers' responses

The 'instant art' series has been developing in response to ideas and suggestions from people who have used earlier titles. We would welcome any comments you might wish to make on existing books, and ideas for additions to the list are always carefully considered.

First published in 2000 in Great Britain by
KEVIN MAYHEW LTD
Buxhall
Stowmarket
Suffolk IP14 3BW

ISBN 1 84003 549 8
Catalogue No 1396074

0 1 2 3 4 5 6 7 8 9

Cover by Kevin Whomes
Printed in Great Britain

Contents

Days of the week 1
Days of the week 2

Christian alphabet 1
Christian alphabet 2

Cover/poster design, Easter
Cover/poster design, Pentecost
Cover/poster design, Christmas

Seasons of the year 1
Seasons of the year 2

Church year 1
Church year 2
Church year 3

Decorative texts

Regular features 1
Regular features 2
Regular features 3
Regular features 4

Worthy workers 1
Worthy workers 2

For the weekly news-sheet 1
For the weekly news-sheet 2

Groups and societies 1
Groups and societies 2
Groups and societies 3
Groups and societies 4

Diary dates and events 1
Diary dates and events 2
Diary dates and events 3
Diary dates and events 4
Diary dates and events 5
Diary dates and events 6

Cartoons 1
Cartoons 2

Proverbs 1
Proverbs 2
Proverbs 3

Crosswords 1
Crosswords 2
Crosswords 3

Wordsearches 1
Wordsearches 2
Wordsearches 3

Activities for children 1
Activities for children 2
Activities for children 3
Activities for children 4

Answers to all puzzles in the last three sections can be found on the reverse of each sheet.

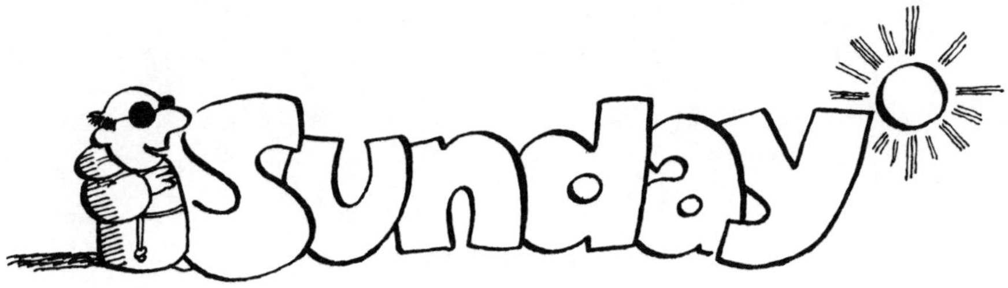
Sunday

Monday

Tuesday

Wednesday

Thursday

Friday

Saturday

SUNDAY

MONDAY

TUESDAY

WEDNESDAY

4:45
THURSDAY

FRIDAY

SATURDAY

Alleluia! Jesus is ALIVE!

BELIEVE in the Lord...

CHRIST is risen!

Start the DAY with Jesus!

God loves EVERYONE!

God is our FATHER!

Jesus is GOOD news!

HAPPY are those who trust in God

Jesus said 'I am with you always'

JESUS is Lord!

KEEP your eyes on God...

LOVE one another...

Faith can MOVE mountains

Jesus said,
'I will NEVER leave you...'

Jesus is the ONLY way...

The PEACE of the Lord
be with you...

Jesus gives QUALITY to your life!

Jesus said, 'I will give you REST...'

Be STRONG in the Lord!

TRUST in the Lord

God loves US all!

Jesus gives us the VICTORY!

Jesus is the WAY!

Jesus is eXtra special!

God loves YOU!

ZZZZ
Sleep well in the Lord...

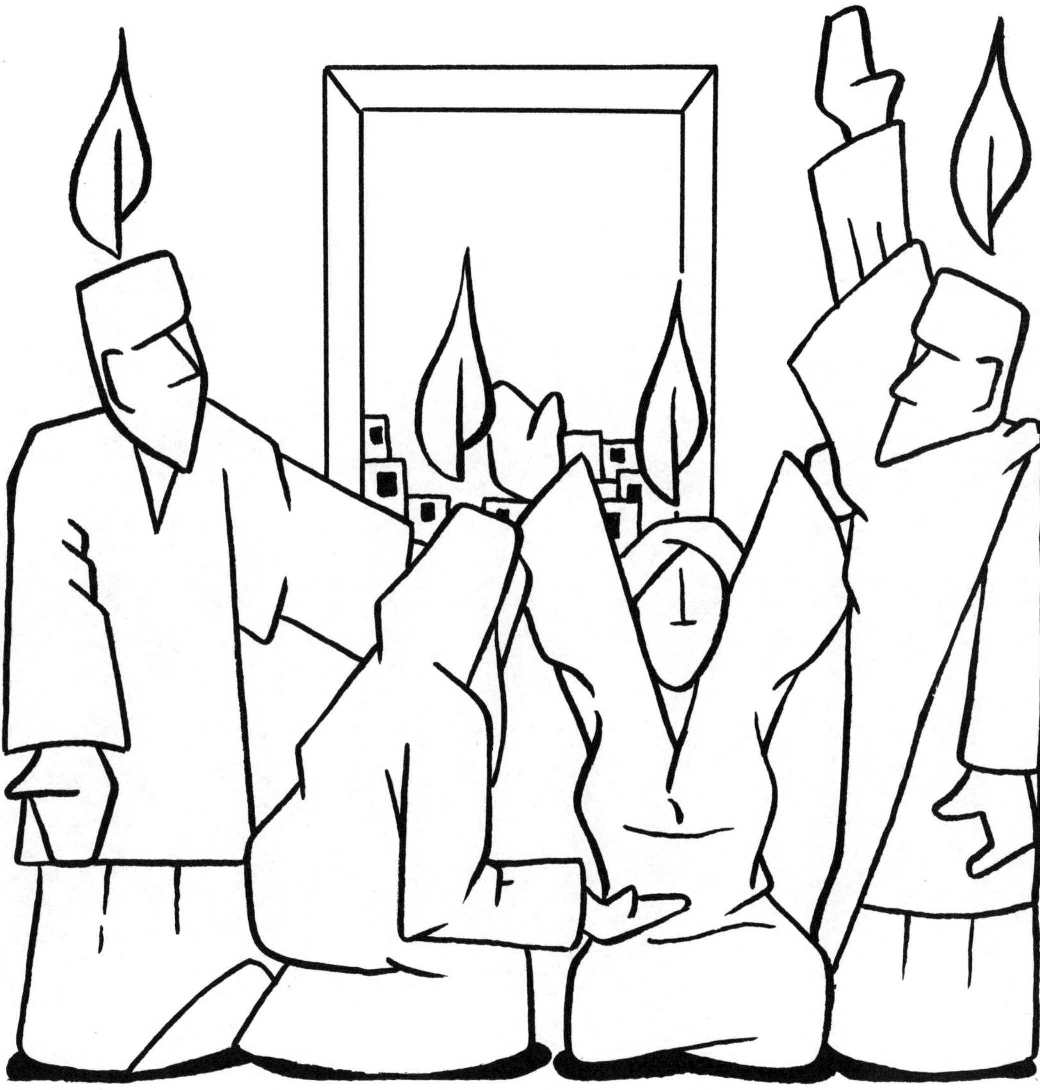

RESERVE
CHRISTMAS TREES
FOR SALE

DIARY
INVITE

MAN SHALL
NOT LIVE BY
BREAD ALONE

I AM
WHO I AM

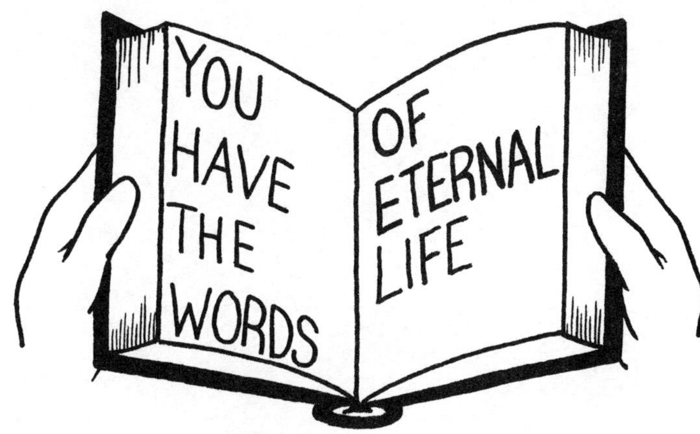
YOU HAVE THE WORDS
OF ETERNAL LIFE

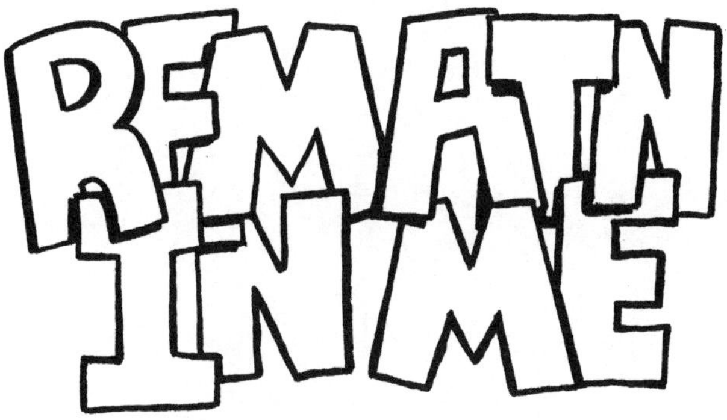
REMAIN
IN ME

PUT ON TH
FULL ARMOU
OF GOD

PRAISE HIM WITH
THE
CLASH
OF
CYMBALS

BLESSED IS
THE MAN WHO
DOES NOT WALK
IN THE COUNSEL
OF THE WICKED...
HE IS LIKE A
TREE PLANTED
BY STREAMS OF WATER

I AM
THE
BREAD
OF LIFE

I
AM
THE
WAY

From the Rector...

The Vicar writes...

FROM the Registers

Mission News

Useful phone numbers

Your letters

WHO's WHO

READERS

Servers

FROM THE PARISH

FROM THE MANSE

THE RECTOR WRITES

THE VICAR WRITES

MISSION NEWS

TREASURER'S REPORT

from the Registers

your letters

Ring! Ring!

READERS

WHO'S WHO
?

STOP PRESS!

SERVERS

NEWS
T

WORD
SEARCHES

CROSSWORD
PUZZLES

TOWN
NEWS

Village
news

Treasurer's
report

STOP
PRESS!

CROSS
WORD
PUZZLES

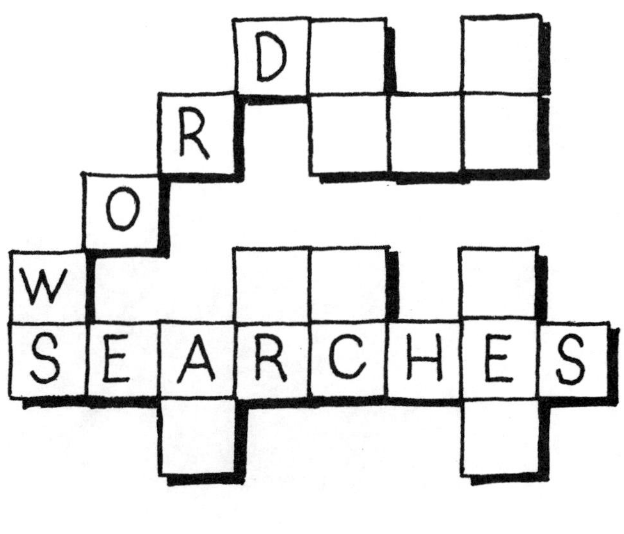
WORD
SEARCHES

CLEANING
ROTA

flower arrangers

BELL RINGERS

Coffee
Rota

CHURCH
YARD
MAINTENANCE

AGENDA
P
C
C

cleaning
rota

Flower
arrangers

BELL
RIN-
GERS

MINE
HIM OVER THERE
HERS
WOT'S IS NAME
?
Coffee rota

Churchyard
maintenance

Parochial Church Council

HYMNS

WEDDING
BELLS

HYMNS
103
416
98
171

INTERCESSIONS

FAMILY SERVICE

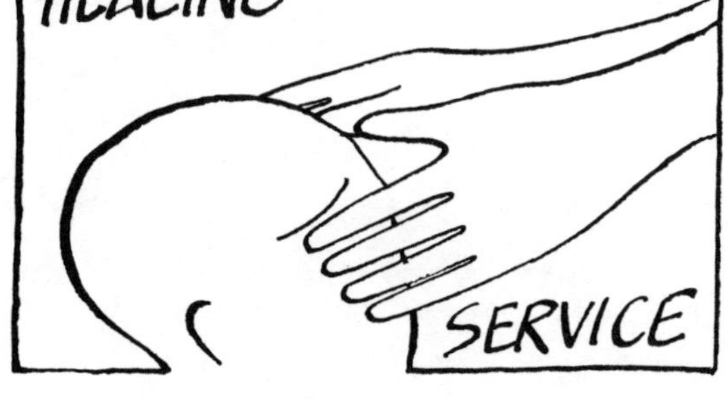
HEALING
SERVICE

3
HOUSE
GROUPS

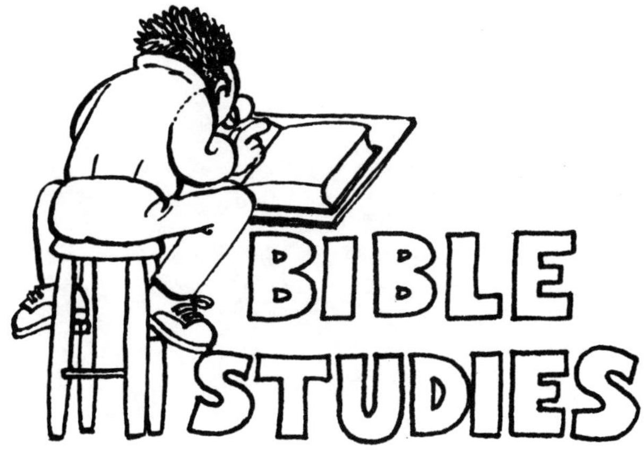
BIBLE
STUDIES

Home
Groups

Prayer
groups

CHILDren's
church

YOUTH
GROUP

CHOIR

Worship
Group

Mums and
toddlers

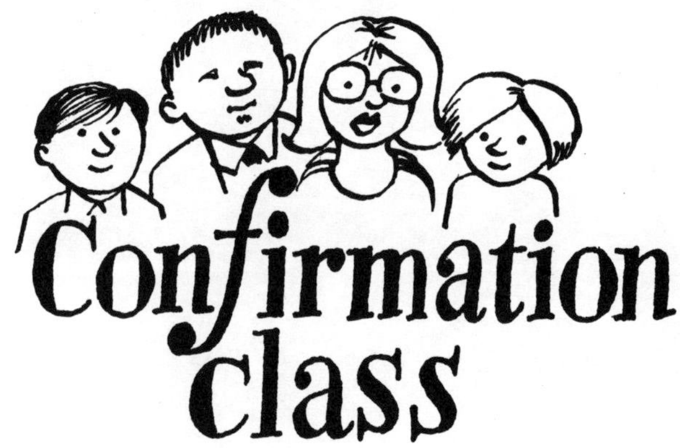
Confirmation
class

First communion class

HOUSE
GROUPS

BIBLE
STUDY
th

PRAYER GROUPS

Children's
Church

YOUTH
GROUP

CHOIR

WORSHIP GROUP

MUMS and TODDLERS
2

first
communion
class

confirmation
class
L
L
L

BONFIRE NIGHT

WHIST DRIVE

BARN DANCE

HARVEST SUPPER

LUNCH CLUB

OVER-SIXTIES
meeting

Christmas Dinner

CHECK POINT
SPONSORED BIKE RIDE

Parish Walk

SLIDE SHOW

WHIST DRIVE

Barn Dance

HARVEST SUPPER

AUTUMN
FAIR

OVER
60s
MEETING

CHRISTMAS
BAZAAR

ALPHABET
SOUP
LUNCH
CLUB

BONFIRE
NIGHT

Christmas
Dinner
S
P

Mon
1st
28th
Sun
Wed
3rd
DIARY DATES
What's on

SPONSORED BIKE RIDE

PARISH WALK

Slide Show

Fundraising

AUTUMN FAIR

Christmas
BAZAAR

Carols by Candlelight

Christingle

Coffee Morning

Mothering Sunday

SUNDAY SCHOOL PARTY

Carols
Carols
CAROLS BY CANDLELIGHT

CHRISTINGLE SERVICE

Coffee Morning
C

SUNDAY SCHOOL PARTY

MOTHERING SUNDAY
To MUM
XXX

DIARY DATES

ROUNDING UP THE ANIMALS - 1
NOAH AND THE BUTTERFLIES

ROUNDING UP THE ANIMALS - 2
NOAH AND THE BEES

ROUNDING UP THE ANIMALS - 3
NOAH AND THE PENGUINS

ROUNDING UP THE ANIMALS - 4
NOAH AND THE DINOSAURS

ROUNDING UP THE ANIMALS-5
NOAH AND THE RABBITS

ROUNDING UP THE ANIMALS-6
NOAH AND THE LESSER BLACK-BACKED GULLS

ROUNDING UP THE ANIMALS - 7
NOAH AND THE CHAMELEONS

ROUNDING UP THE ANIMALS - 8
NOAH AND THE TORTOISES

If people don't know what's impossible...
2
4
..They'll do it!

THE CHURCH EXISTS NOT ONLY TO COMFORT THE DISTURBED...
OI!
BOOT
BUT TO DISTURB THE COMFORTABLE!

GOD WANTS SPIRITUAL FRUITS
NOT RELIGIOUS NUTS!

A CHAIN IS NO STRONGER
THAN ITS WEAKEST LINK

SERVE THE LORD...
THE PAY ISN'T MUCH BUT THE RETIREMENT BENEFITS
ARE OUT OF THIS WORLD

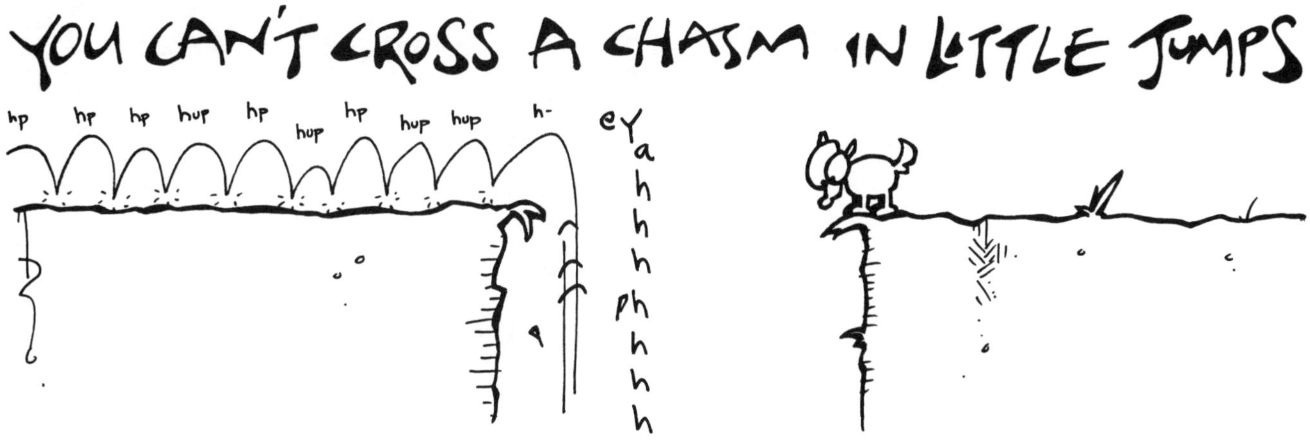
YOU CAN'T CROSS A CHASM IN LITTLE JUMPS

THE MAN WHO STICKS TO THE MIDDLE OF THE ROAD IS SOONER OR LATER GOING TO GET KNOCKED DOWN

God often visits us...
Yoweeee it's me
but most of the time we're not at home

Nov 02
JAN 06

CROSSWORD ON THE APOSTLE PAUL

ACROSS
5. On one missionary journey, Paul had a vision at Troas telling him to go across to this place (Acts 16:9).
6. This group of people were constantly trying to oppose Paul (Acts 9:23).
7. This man was sent to restore Paul's sight (Acts 9:11-12).
9. When Paul spoke to the people of Athens 'his ideas were strange to their _ _ _ _' (Acts 17:20).
12. Paul was raised at this Doctor of the Law's feet (Acts 22:3).
13. Paul was stoned at this place on his first missionary journey (Acts 14:8-19).
15. Paul was blinded on the road to this place (Acts 22:11; 26:12).

DOWN
1. He accompanied Paul on his first missionary journey (Acts 13:2).
2. The deputy of Paphos who became a believer after Paul preached to him (Acts 13:7).
3. Paul shaved his head, having taken one (Acts 18:18).
4. Paul was bitten by one of these, but suffered no harm (Acts 28:3-5).
8. Aquila and Priscilla sailed with Paul to this place after he had shaved his head in Cenchrea (Acts 18:18).
10. Paul appealed to this chief governor in Rome (Acts 26:32).
11. She was a seller of purple goods in Philippi (Acts 16:13-34).
14. Paul was also known by this name (Acts 13:9).

Now take the letters in the lightly shaded boxes and unscramble to find the name of the silversmith's head in Ephesus who led an uprising against Paul:

....

JAN 03

GENERAL CROSSWORD NO.1

ACROSS
1. To drink water like a dog (Judges 7:5).
5. This king had his life prolonged by 15 years after he prayed to God for longevity (Isaiah 38:5).
7. The son of Boaz and Ruth (Ruth 4:17).
8. Gideon saved the Israelites from oppression by the people of this land (Judges 6:14).
11. Aquila and Priscilla expounded the way of God more fully to this Jew at Ephesus (Acts 18:24-26).
14. David ate the shewbread at this city (1 Samuel 21:1-6).
15. One of Noah's sons (Genesis 5:32).
16. Mary poured this ointment over Christ before his death, while he was in the house of Simon the leper (Mark 14:3).

DOWN
1. One of the twelve sons of Jacob, who formed the priestly tribe (Numbers 1:49-50).
2. Paul wrote an epistle to the believers at this Macedonian city (Acts 16:12).
3. One of the four 'major prophets', who prophesied during the reign of Jehoiachin.
4. One of the five cities of the Philistines, through which the ark of God travelled (1 Samuel 5:10).
6. A son of Adam, slain by Cain (Genesis 4:25).
9. A famous woman of the Bible, who redeemed the Jews from death at the hands of Haman.
10. Ruth's mother-in-law (Ruth 1:4-8).
12. Jacob's uncle, father of Rachel and Leah (Genesis 29:10).
13. Jesus told his disciples to drink from the _ _ _ which symbolised the blood of the covenant (Matthew 26:27).

ANSWERS

CROSSWORD ON THE APOSTLE PAUL

ACROSS:

5. Macedonia	6. Jews	7. Ananias	9. Ears
12. Gamaliel	13. Lystra	15. Damascus	

DOWN:

1. Barnabas	2. Sergius Paulus	3. Vow	4. Viper
8. Syria	10. Caesar	11. Lydia	14. Saul

The name of the silversmith = Demetrius

GENERAL CROSSWORD NO.1

ACROSS:

1. Lap	5. Hezekiah	7. Obed	8. Midian
11. Apollos	14. Nob	15. Ham	16. Pure nard

DOWN:

1. Levi	2. Philippi	3. Ezekiel	4. Ekron
6. Abel	9. Esther	10. Naomi	12. Laban
13. Cup			

Oct. 02

GENERAL CROSSWORD NO.2

ACROSS

2. When Lot hesitated, the angels '_ _ _ _ _ ed' his hand to pull him from Sodom (Genesis 19:16).
6. This King had 1000 wives and concubines (I Kings 11:3).
8. He was called Satan once by Christ (Matthew 16:23).
10. One of Noah's sons (Genesis 5:32).
12. A New Testament epistle of uncertain authorship.
14. National god of the Philistines (Judges 16:23).
16. He 'walked with God' (Genesis 6:9).
17. David fled once to this King of Gath (I Samuel 21:10).
18. We are told to bear Christ's reproach and join him outside the _____ (Hebrews 13:13).
19. Moses held these aloft to ensure Israel's victory over the Amalekites in battle (Exodus 17:12).
20. He was 'translated that he should not see death' (Hebrews 11:5).

DOWN

1. Balaam's spoke to him (Numbers 22:28).
3. We are the clay and God is the _______ (Isaiah 64:8).
4. Christ was 'a man of ________ and acquainted with grief' (Isaiah 53:3).
5. He was swallowed by a big fish.
7. One of the sacrificial creatures under the Mosaic law (Numbers 5:8).
9. He was thrown into a fiery furnace (Daniel 3:23).
11. Father of the Jews (Luke 3:8).
13. One of the King's chamberlains in the book of Esther (Esther 6:2).
15. 'The birds of the air have _____; but the Son of Man hath not where to lay his head' (Matthew 8:20).
18. Christ turned water into wine at this place (John 2:11).

CROSSWORD ON BOOKS OF THE BIBLE

The grid below contains the names of 24 Books of the Bible, and some letters have been entered to give you a start. Can you fill in the missing letters to complete the grid?

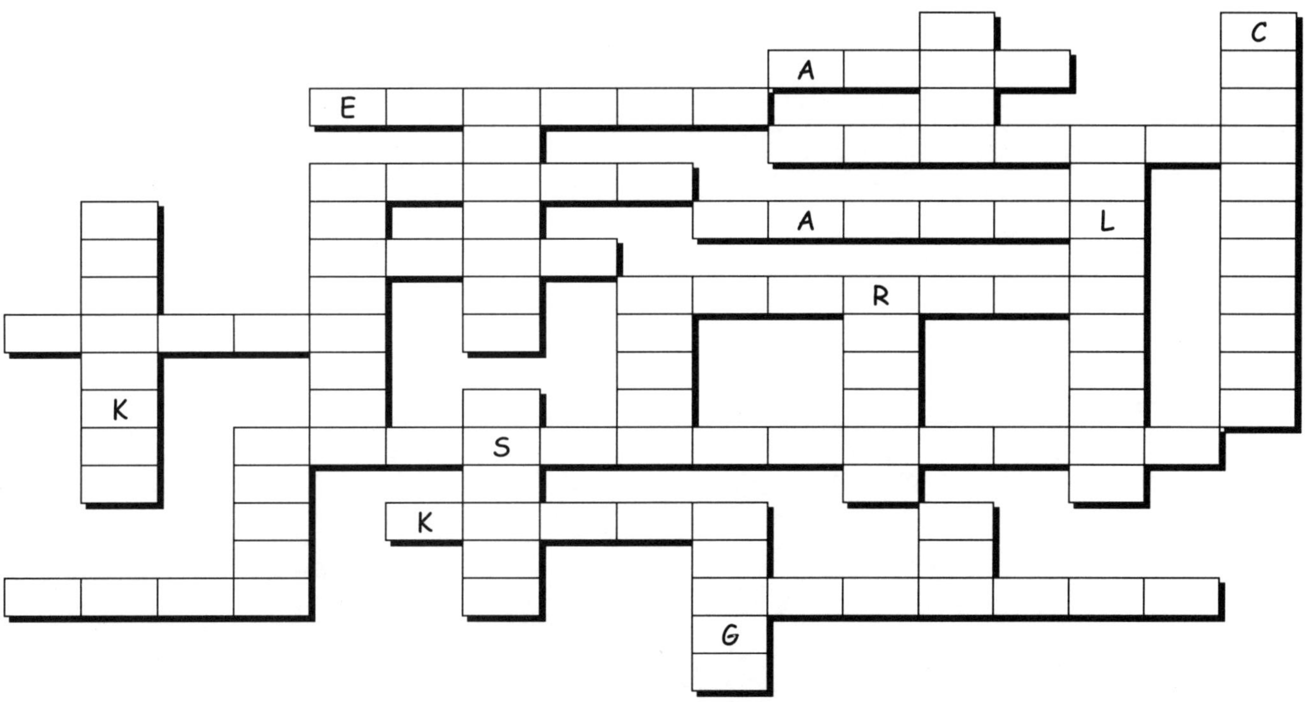

ANSWERS

GENERAL CROSSWORD NO.2

ACROSS:

2. Grasp
6. Solomon
8. Peter
10. Ham
12. Hebrews
14. Dagon
16. Noah
17. Achish
18. Camp
19. Hands
20. Enoch

DOWN:

1. Ass
3. Potter
4. Sorrows
5. Jonah
7. Ram
9. Shadrach
11. Abraham
13. Bigthana
15. Nests
18. Cana

CROSSWORD ON BOOKS OF THE BIBLE

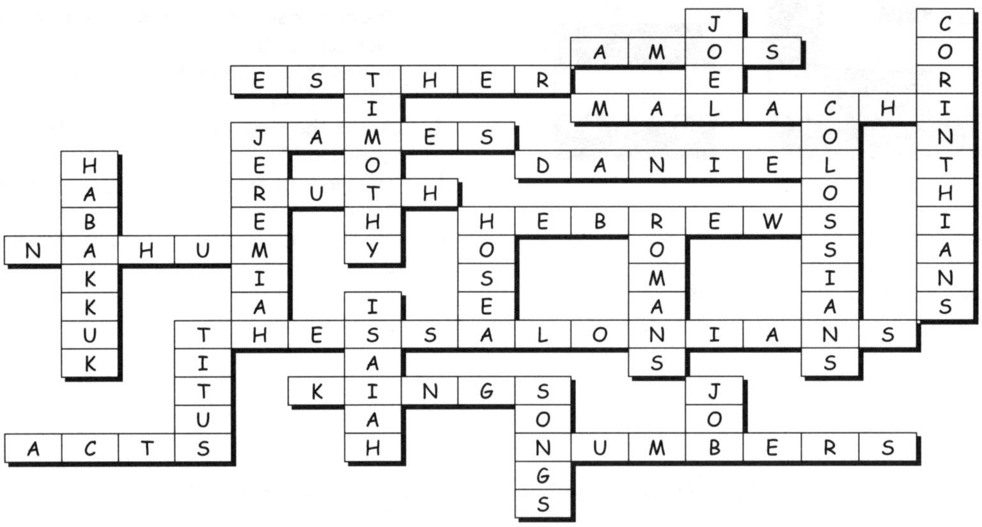

Used Dec 02

GENERAL CROSSWORD NO.3

ACROSS
1. Third book of the Bible containing the Law.
6. One of the 'minor' prophets.
7. The body of saints are sometimes described as this female character (Revelation 21:9).
9. What does God own on a thousand hills? (Psalm 50:10).
10. The chief of Saul's herdsmen, an Edomite (1 Samuel 21:7).
12. The name Naomi gave herself upon her return to Israel (Ruth 1:20).
14. The father of Abraham (Genesis 11:26).
15. 'The Lord our God is ___ Lord' (Deuteronomy 6:4).
16. One of Jacob's sons (Genesis 30:11).

DOWN
1. Father of Noah (Genesis 5:30).
2. The wife of Xerxes before Esther (Esther 1:11).
3. Gog is described as being the chief prince of this place (Ezekiel 39:1).
4. He killed Abel (Genesis 4:8).
5. The first preacher of Christianity to be killed after Christ's death (Acts 7:59).
8. The plagues happened here (Exodus 10:12).
10. The fifth son of Jacob (Genesis 30:6).
11. The head of Nebuchadnezzar's image was made of this metal (Daniel 2:32).
13. This imparts wisdom (Proverbs 29:15).

CROSSWORD ON WOMEN OF THE BIBLE

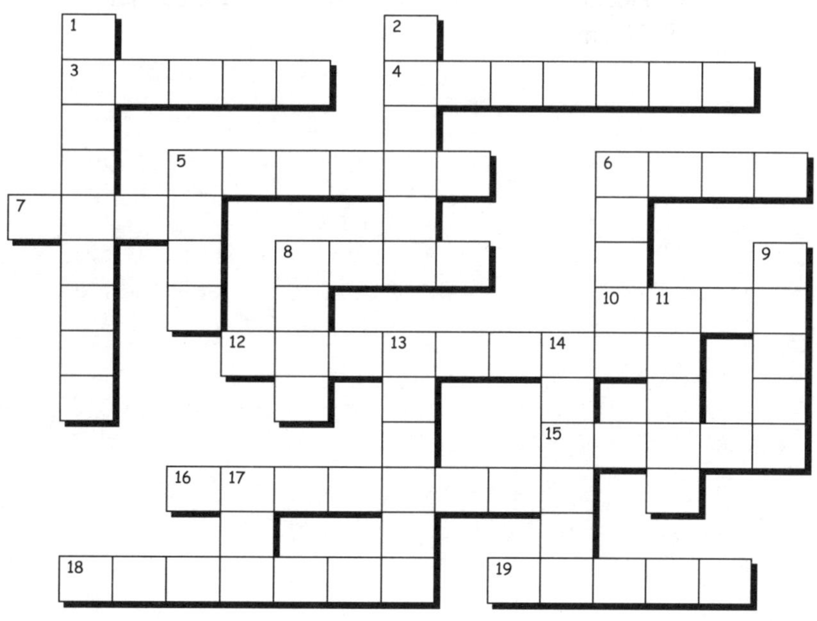

ACROSS
3. A seller of purple in Thyatira (Acts 16:14).
4. She became one of David's wives after her husband died (1 Samuel 25:37-42).
5. Sister to Lazarus (John 11:1).
6. Wife of Boaz.
7. Naomi renamed herself this after her husband and sons died (Ruth 1:20).
8. Timothy's faithful grandmother (2 Timothy 1:5).
10. A prophetess who met the newborn Jesus (Luke 2:36).
12. Mother of Solomon (I Kings 2:13).
15. David's daughter, violated by Amnon and avenged by Absalom (2 Samuel 13:22).
16. Elkanah, father of Samuel, had her to wife (1 Samuel 1:2).
18. Daughter of Bethuel and Isaac's wife (Genesis 24:67).
19. One of Naomi's daughters-in-law (Ruth 1:14).

DOWN
1. Mother of John the Baptist (Luke 1:13).
2. Esther succeeded her as Queen (Esther 1:19).
5. Christ's mother (Matthew 13:55).
6. She concealed the two Israelite spies sent into Jericho by Joshua (Joshua 6:17).
8. First wife of Jacob (Genesis 29:23).
9. Sarah's Egyptian handmaid who gave birth to Ishmael (Genesis 16:15).
11. Wife of Elimelech, mother of Mahlon and Chilion (Ruth 1:2).
13. Mother of Samuel (1 Samuel 1:20).
14. The book between Nehemiah and Job.
17. The first woman (I Timothy 2:13).

ANSWERS

GENERAL CROSSWORD NO.3

ACROSS:

1. Leviticus	6. Amos	7. Bride	9. Cattle
10. Doeg	12. Mara	14. Terah	15. One
16. Gad			

DOWN:

1. Lamech	2. Vashti	3. Tubal	4. Cain
5. Stephen	8. Egypt	10. Dan	11. Gold
13. Rod			

CROSSWORD ON WOMEN OF THE BIBLE

ACROSS:

3. Lydia	4. Abigail	5. Martha	6. Ruth
7. Mara	8. Lois	10. Anna	12. Bathsheba
15. Tamar	16. Peninnah	18. Rebekah	19. Orpah

DOWN:

1. Elisabeth	2. Vashti	5. Mary	6. Rahab
8. Leah	9. Hagar	13. Hannah	14. Esther
17. Eve	19. Naomi		

WORDSEARCH - BIBLE GEMS

FIND THE FOLLOWING GEMS IN THE GRID BELOW:

Jasper	Sapphire	Chalcedony	Emerald
Sardonyx	Sardius	Carbuncle	Topaz
Diamond	Amethyst	Agate	Ligure
Onyx	Beryl		

C	A	R	B	U	N	C	L	E	S
S	H	R	E	P	S	A	J	A	T
D	L	A	R	E	M	E	P	Z	S
I	I	P	L	R	I	P	L	A	Y
A	G	L	K	C	H	O	R	P	H
M	U	Y	E	I	E	D	G	O	T
O	R	R	R	T	I	D	X	T	E
N	E	E	M	U	A	Y	O	J	M
D	T	B	S	Q	N	G	N	N	A
F	X	Y	N	O	D	R	A	S	Y

ANSWERS

WORDSEARCH - BIBLE GEMS

C	A	R	B	U	N	C	L	E	S
S	H	R	E	P	S	A	J	A	T
D	L	A	R	E	M	E	P	Z	S
I	I	P	L	R	I	P	L	A	Y
A	G	L	K	C	H	O	R	P	H
M	U	Y	E	I	E	D	G	O	T
O	R	R	R	T	I	D	X	T	E
N	E	E	M	U	A	Y	O	J	M
D	T	B	S	Q	N	G	N	N	A
F	X	Y	N	O	D	R	A	S	Y

WORDSEARCH - KINGS OF ISRAEL AND JUDAH

FIND THE FOLLOWING KINGS IN THE GRID BELOW:

Jeroboam	Menahem	Ahab	Elah
Jehoahaz	Manasseh	Jotham	Zedekiah
Asa	Joram	Amon	

J	O	T	H	A	M	M	H
E	E	C	V	H	A	A	E
H	Q	R	E	R	I	G	S
O	Y	L	O	K	L	T	S
A	A	J	E	B	A	H	A
H	D	D	D	F	O	S	N
A	E	P	N	O	M	A	A
Z	M	E	H	A	N	E	M

ANSWERS

WORDSEARCH - KINGS OF ISRAEL AND JUDAH

J	O	T	H	A	M	M	H
E	E	C	V	H	A	A	E
H	Q	R	E	R	I	G	S
O	Y	L	O	K	L	T	S
A	A	J	E	B	A	H	A
H	D	D	D	F	O	S	N
A	E	P	N	O	M	A	A
Z	M	E	H	A	N	E	M

WORDSEARCH - ANIMALS OF THE BIBLE

FIND THE FOLLOWING BIBLICAL ANIMALS
IN THE GRID BELOW:

Bullock	Sheep	Cow	Horse
Ram	Goat	Ox	Ass
Bear	Camel	Deer	Dog
Elephant	Ferret	Fox	Hare
Leopard	Lion	Wolf	

F	E	R	R	E	T	K	P	F	E
L	J	P	S	H	C	U	L	L	S
E	E	W	E	O	O	O	E	I	R
M	V	O	L	E	W	P	X	O	O
A	Q	L	P	T	H	B	R	N	H
C	U	F	M	A	S	S	A	K	A
B	O	A	N	O	R	E	E	D	R
X	R	T	C	G	O	D	B	F	E

ANSWERS

WORDSEARCH - ANIMALS OF THE BIBLE

F	E	R	R	E	T	K	P	F	E
L	J	P	S	H	C	U	L	L	S
E	E	W	E	O	O	O	E	I	R
M	V	O	L	E	W	P	X	O	O
A	Q	L	P	T	H	B	R	N	H
C	U	F	M	A	S	S	A	K	A
B	O	A	N	O	R	E	E	D	R
X	R	T	C	G	O	D	B	F	E

IN PSALM 150 WE ARE TOLD TO PRAISE GOD ON A VARIETY OF MUSICAL INSTRUMENTS. CAN YOU FILL THEIR NAMES IN TO THE GRID BELOW, USING THE COUPLE OF LETTERS THAT HAVE BEEN PUT IN TO HELP YOU?

IN EACH OF THE SETS OF NAMES BELOW, ONE IS THAT OF A PRIEST. CAN YOU CIRCLE THE CORRECT NAME, THEN ANSWER THE QUESTIONS BELOW?

1. CALEB	CHRIST	CAIN	CAESAR
2. ELIAB	ESTHER	ESAU	ELI
3. ANNA	AARON	ADAM	ABEL
4. ELIMELECH	ELAH	EZEKIEL	ELIEZER
5. POTIPHERAH	PAUL	POTIPHAR	PRISCILLA
6. ZEBULUN	ZADOK	ZACCHAEUS	ZIBA
7. JEMIMA	JAMES	JETHRO	JESSE
8. ENOCH	ELKANAH	EBENEZER	EZRA

Which was the priest of On (Genesis 41:45)? ....

Which was the priest of Midian (Exodus 18:1)? ....

Which is our Great High Priest,
the most important of all (Hebrews 4:14; 9:11)? ....

THE WORD WHICH HAS BEEN SCRAMBLED UP BELOW FORMS A MAIN THEME IN THE BOOK OF PHILEMON. 1) SEE IF YOU CAN UNSCRAMBLE THE WORD, THEN 2) TRY TO MAKE AS MANY WORDS OF THREE LETTERS OR MORE AS YOU CAN FROM IT.

ANSWERS

INSTRUMENTS

		C	Y	M	B	A	L	S	
F								T	
L	Y	R	E		T			R	
U					R			I	
T	A	M	B	O	U	R	I	N	E
E					M			G	
		H	A	R	P			S	
					E				
					T				

PRIESTS

Christ, Eli, Aaron, Ezekiel, Potipherah, Zadok, Jethro, Ezra.
Priest of On = Potipherah; Priest of Midian = Jethro; Great High Priest = Christ.

PHILEMON

Scrambled word = FORGIVENESS

Draw two identical baskets, cutting a 'door' in one if them. Stick them together round the edges, open the door and place inside 5 paper loaves and 2 paper fishes, to show the food Jesus used to feed the multitude.

In Matthew 13, Jesus compared the Kingdom of God to hidden treasure. Unscramble the words below to discover some of the other things he likened it to.

ASYTE

LPRAE

ENT

SSTDDMAUREE

Above you will see pictures of some of the things God created on days two, three, four, five and six of creation.
Look in Genesis 1 to find out which picture - A, B, C, D, or E - goes with which day.

Day 2 ....

Day 3 ....

Day 4 ....

Day 5 ....

Day 6 ....

ANSWERS

MATTHEW 13 - KINGDOM OF GOD

Scrambled words are - YEAST (verse 33); NET (verse 47); PEARL (verse 45); and MUSTARD SEED (verse 31).

DAYS OF CREATION

Day 2=D; Day 3=E; Day 4=B; Day 5=A; Day 6=C.

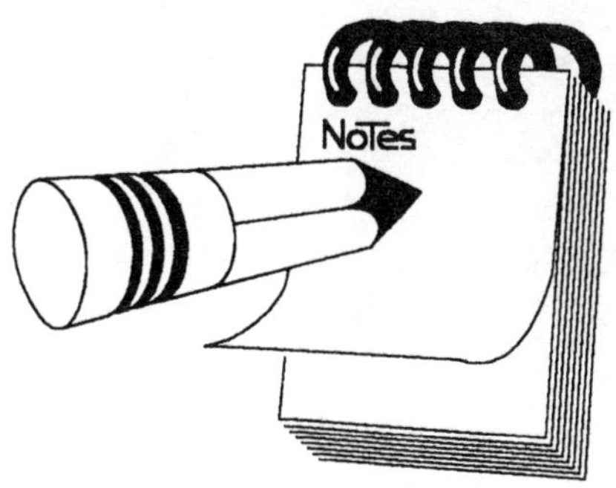

Write the alphabet down the side of a large piece of paper, then try to find a biblical person, place or word for each letter, e.g. B = Bethany, Y = Yoke.

Unscramble the names of these Old Testament books and then write them in the order they appear in the Bible.

LSSMPA
DEGJUS
AAMHLIC
ZLKEEIE
SXUOED
AEEHMHIN

1. ....
2. ....
3. ....
4. ....
5. ....
6. ....

Draw lines to link together the husbands and wives among the names below.

HANNAH ZECHARIAH JACOB
AQUILA EVE
ADAM REBEKAH
JEZEBEL ANANIAS
PRISCILLA ELKANAH RACHEL SARAH
ABRAHAM AHAB ISAAC ELIZABETH
SAPPHIRA
RUTH DAVID BOAZ BATHSHEBA

ANSWERS

OLD TESTAMENT BOOKS

Exodus, Judges, Nehemiah, Psalms, Ezekiel, Malachi

HUSBANDS AND WIVES

Elkanah and Hannah
Ananias and Sapphira
Isaac and Rebekah
Zechariah and Elizabeth
Adam and Eve
Ahab and Jezebel
Abraham and Sarah
Jacob and Rachel
Boaz and Ruth
David and Bathsheba
Aquila and Priscilla.

Can you name the people linked with FIRE in the Bible from the following clues:

A burning bush .... Exodus 3:1-10
Snake bite! .... Acts 28:5
A chariot bound skyward .... 2 Kings 2:11
Fire from a rock .... Judges 6:21
A fiery furnace .... Daniel 3:20
Vision of a great fire .... Amos 7:4-5

Solve the following clues to make a famous Bible quotation:

 ~~R~~ = H ~~E~~ _ _ _

 ~~G~~ = RD _ _ _ _

 ~~F~~ ~~H~~ _ _

 ~~E~~ = M ~~E~~ _ _

 ~~E~~ _ _ _ _ +  ~~ART~~ = RD _ _ _ _

 Use 1st letter only _

 ~~B~~ = SH _ _ _ _ _

 ~~ES~~ _ _ _

 ~~TCH~~ = NT _ _ _ _

= ....
....
....

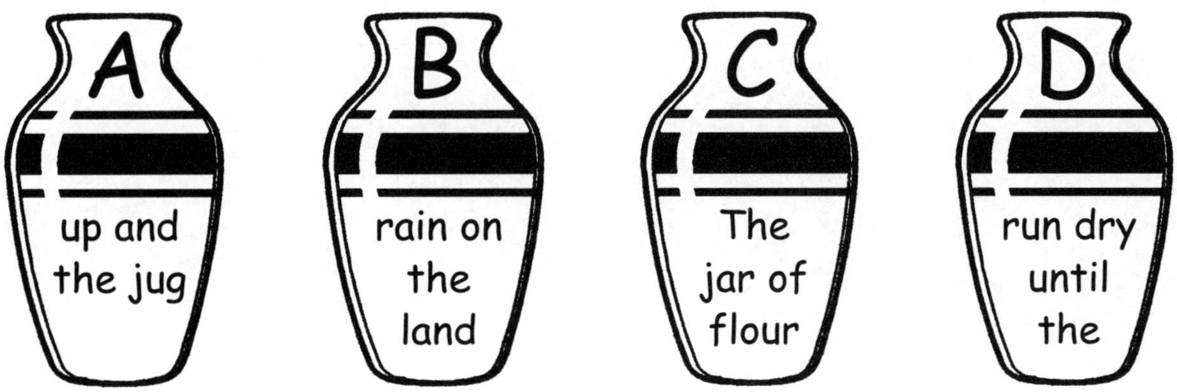

Place the pots of oil in the correct order to show the words spoken to the widow of Zarephath by Elijah

ANSWERS

FIRE

Bush = Moses (Exodus 3:1-10)
Snake = Paul (Acts 28:5)
Chariot = Elijah (2 Kings 2:11)
Rock = Gideon (Judges 6:21)
Furnace = Shadrach, Meshach & Abednego (Daniel 3:20)
Vision = Amos (Amos 7:4-5).

FAMOUS QUOTATION

'The Lord is my shepherd; I shall not want' (Psalm 23).

ELIJAH'S WORDS TO THE WIDOW OF ZAREPHATH

'The jar of flour will not be used up and the jug of oil will not run dry until the day the Lord gives rain on the land' (1 Kings 17:14). Order of pots of oil = C, G, A, E, D, F, B.